Luke
M gan.

CW01637150

WHEN WILL MY BABY BRAIN FALL OUT?

WRITTEN AND ILLUSTRATED
BY MARTIN BAXENDALE

Text and illustrations © copyright
Martin Baxendale 2007

Published by Laugh Out Loud Books,
an imprint of Silent But Deadly
Publications, 21 Bisley Road,
Stroud, Glos., GL5 1HF

Printed in England by
Stoate & Bishop Printers Ltd,
Shaftesbury Industrial Centre,
Cheltenham, Glos. GL51 9NH

All rights reserved. No part of this
book may be reproduced, stored in a
retrieval system or trasmitted in any
form or by any means, electronic,
mechanical, photocopying, recording
or otherwise, without the prior
permission of the publishers and
copyright holder.

ISBN: 978-0-9550500-6-0

For Rosie, Misho and Zuza,
with lots and lots
of love.

"It's too difficult, Mum! I don't understand it! Help me, Mum! Help me, please!"

Millie, like many seven-year-olds, struggled a bit with her maths homework. Actually, she struggled a lot, and she always complained very, very loudly about it. So Mum had heard all this whining and whinging lots and lots of times before.

What Mum *hadn't* heard before was what Millie said next:

"Mum? When will my baby brain fall out?"

At first Mum thought she hadn't heard properly.

"Sorry, Millie. What was that? I wasn't listening. I thought you said something about your *brain* falling out!"

"Yes, how long will it be before my baby brain falls out and my big-girl brain grows instead? Then I'll understand my maths homework and do it in no time at all. And have lots more time left over to play and watch TV!"

Mum looked up from her newspaper and smiled at Millie across the big wooden kitchen table.

"Millie, sweetie, your brain isn't going to…"

There was a burst of noise from the sitting room as someone switched on the television then turned the volume down a bit. Millie looked over her shoulder and listened, but it wasn't the sound of the programme that she was waiting for. So she started drawing a fairy beside the unfinished sums on her homework paper.

As she drew, Millie told Mum how her big brother Alfie had kindly explained to her all about baby brains and grown-up brains (and their different abilities to cope with maths homework) in that special caring and helpful way that only big brothers aged nine-and-a-half are capable of:

"Alfie said I can't do maths 'cos I've only got a stupid little baby brain. But he said *he* can do maths easy peasy 'cos he's got a grown-up big-boy brain. And it's much huger and more intelligent than my silly little pea-size baby brain."

Mum frowned, put down her newspaper and leaned across the table.

"Well it was very silly of Alfie to say that. Of *course* you don't have a stupid little..."

Millie, who had been concentrating on the fairy drawing, looked up with a big smile.

"But it's okay! Don't worry! I'm growing up really fast. I've grown lots and lots this year and I'm almost the biggest girl in my class now. So my baby brain *will* fall out soon won't it? Just like my baby teeth keep going all wobbly and falling out. Then my big-girl brain will grow instead. Just like grown-up teeth come in place of baby teeth after they fall out."

Millie put down her pencil, placed the tip of her finger against the side of her head and pushed. Then she let her head wobble from side to side, her smile getting bigger and bigger.

"I think my baby brain's getting wobbly already. I bet it's going to fall out any day now! Then I'll get my grown-up, big-girl brain that can do maths and understand Alfie's jokes."

Mum stared, her mouth wide open and a bewildered expression on her face. She was trying to think of something to say in reply to this obviously very daft idea. But somehow the sheer daftness of the whole thing had made her temporarily speechless.

In the sitting room the television was suddenly turned up loud again. Millie looked around and started to slide off her chair. As she headed for the kitchen door, she glanced at Mum, who was still sitting at the table with her mouth open.

"Mum, will the Brain Fairy come and take

SNORE!
MONEY
Will the Brain Fairy come and take my baby brain away?

my baby brain away, just like the Tooth Fairy takes my baby teeth? I get fifty pence for a baby tooth. But I've got lots of baby teeth and only one baby brain. I think I should get a lot more than fifty pence for my baby brain, don't you? How much do you think a baby brain is worth?"

Mum slowly shook her head.

"I…I don't know, Millie. I suppose…hang on! Millie! Come back here! Seriously, your brain really isn't going to…"

But Millie was gone. She was off down the hall to the sitting room where her brother Alfie was sprawled on the sofa with the remote control, shouting: "Millie! Millie!! Hurry up, slowcoach! The Simpsons are on! You're missing it!"

The next day was a Saturday, so there would be no more school for Millie and Alfie until after the weekend. Which Millie was very glad about because by bedtime she still hadn't managed to finish her maths homework. Not even with first Dad and then Mum trying to help. No matter how much they tried to explain the problems to her, she just couldn't seem to get the hang of half of them.

Even Alfie's advice, which went something like "Good grief, Millie! Anyone with *half* a baby brain could do those sums", didn't seem to help much.

In fact it made her want to shove her rubber up his nose.

So it was just as well for Alfie that he was on his way out to the car. Dad was taking him to a sleep-over at Alfie's friend's house, and by the time Millie had found her rubber and was looking for a nose to jam it up, they'd gone.

When Millie and Mum had finally given up and put the unfinished homework away in a drawer, Mum once again tried to explain that Millie's brain really *wasn't* going to go all wobbly and fall out. And that a more grown-up, cleverer one, better at doing maths, really *wasn't* going to suddenly grow in its place.

But Millie wasn't listening. She'd already got a notepad out and was writing a letter to the Brain Fairy, asking her to please be prepared for an urgent brain-collecting visit to Millie's bedroom. Because Millie was sure her baby brain felt really quite wobbly and would be falling out and ready for collection very soon indeed.

"Dear Brane Furry,"she wrote (unfortunately Millie often had trouble with spellings as well as with maths) "pleaz look in my bedrum evrey nite to see if my baby brane is redy for collekshun. I think it wil be very soon. Bi the way, mi baby brane is probbly wurth as much munny as all mi baby teath put toogether, so…"

Millie looked up at Mum, who'd just finished explaining what *really* happens with brains as children get older. How they learn more and understand more as they grow up, rather than their baby brains simply falling out.

"Mum! How many baby teeth do I have? Can you count them for me?"

Mum realised Millie hadn't heard a word she'd just said to her. She sighed, leaned across the table and said:

"Open your mouth…wider…one, two, three, four, five, six...ouch! You bit me! Very funny! Open up again. Seven, eight, nine, ten, eleven, twelve…"

When Mum had finished counting, Millie started trying to work out just how much all of her baby teeth were worth, at 50p each. And then how much she should ask the Brain Fairy to give her for her baby brain if that was worth the same as all her baby teeth put together. But of course she was still having problems with her maths:

"So that's fifty pence times…hmmm…so that equals…ummm…"

Millie frowned as she tried to do the (really quite large) sum.

"...okay, let's just call it eight pounds ninety five pence. That's a nice round number." (which was something she'd heard grown-ups say).

"Yes, eight pounds ninety five pence, that's what I'll ask for." (which was exactly the price of a new Bratz doll that she'd seen in a shop last week and really, really wanted to get).

"I'm sure the Brain Fairy can afford that. After all, if she's a Brain Fairy, she must be quite brainy and clever. Which means she must get paid quite a lot. So she must have plenty of money. Okay, now I'll leave this here on the table with a nice snack. Dad? Can you help me make a midnight snack for the Brain Fairy before I go to bed? Like we do when Father Christmas is coming?"

Dad, who had just come into the kitchen and was cleaning the top of the cooker before starting on the washing up, glanced over his shoulder at Millie, puzzled.

"Huh? Brain Fairy? What Brain Fairy!?"

He gave Mum a 'What's going on?' sort of look, and she whispered in his ear:

"I'll explain later. Just play along and help Millie make the snack."

As Millie poured a glass of milk for the Brain Fairy, Dad opened a jar of sardine paste.

"A sardine sandwich should be a perfect snack for the Brain Fairy," said Millie, buttering the bread dad had sliced for her. "Grandma says

sardines are good brain food. She says they help make you cleverer."

Millie was sure the Brain Fairy would appreciate being left a snack that was good for the brain. Just as the Tooth Fairy would no doubt be very impressed by being left a snack that was good for the teeth, like a nice crunchy carrot.

Not that Millie had ever actually left a midnight snack when the Tooth Fairy was coming. But that wasn't the point. The point was (as she explained to Mum) that her baby brain falling out was a much bigger deal than just a little baby tooth falling out.

And anyway, having to carry loads of heavy baby brains around all night was bound to be much harder work for the Brain Fairy than just collecting up teensy baby teeth was for the Tooth Fairy.

So it probably made the Brain Fairy very hungry. Plus (though she didn't tell Mum this bit) she really did want that new Bratz doll very much indeed. And she hoped that the Brain Fairy might be a little more generous with the money after a nice snack and a glass of cold milk. As an after-thought, she added a few crisps to the plate with the sandwich…and an apple from the fruit bowl…two bananas…an orange…three chocolate biscuits…and…

"Millie! That's enough," said Mum. "Put that cake tin back in the cupboard. The Brain Fairy will never eat all that. And if Grandma says sardine sandwiches are good brain food and make you cleverer, then maybe *you* should eat them more often."

"It might help you with your maths and spellings, Millie," added Mum, nudging Dad with her elbow.

"What? Oh, yes," agreed Dad. "Granny's right, oily fish like sardines really are supposed to be good for your brain. It's been scientifically proven. I read it somewhere."

Millie just smiled at them both.

"I don't need to. When my baby brain falls out and I get my grown-up brain instead, I'll be as clever as Alfie!"

After Mum had chased Millie upstairs to clean her teeth and get ready for bed, Dad looked at the plate full of food, scratched his head and said:

"Brain Fairy? Baby brain falling out? Alfie clever?! What on earth is going on? You know, I'm actually quite peckish. Do you want that sandwich or can I...?"

Mum shook her head, so Dad sat down and started munching the Brain Fairy's sardine sandwich and crisps.

"You'd better not let Millie catch you scoffing that," said Mum. "She's quite serious about all this. I'll just go and tuck her in, then I'll explain it all to you. And leave some of those crisps for me."

Upstairs, Millie had cleaned her teeth, got into her pyjamas and snuggled into bed all on her own without even having to be nagged. The bedroom light was already off, so Mum tiptoed carefully across the toy-cluttered carpet to kiss her good night.

"Millie, stop that! I can't kiss you! I keep missing!" complained Mum as Millie rocked her head from side to side on her pillow. "Keep still! I've kissed your *pillow* twice now!"

Millie stopped just long enough for Mum to kiss her.

Then she started rocking her head again, even faster.

"I'm trying to loosen my baby brain a bit and

make it wobblier, so it'll fall out quicker. Night, night, Mum," said Millie.

Mum sat down on the end of the bed.

"Um, Millie sweetie? How do you think your um…baby brain is going to fall out exactly? Where's it going to come out of?"

"Oh, Mum! Don't be silly! You know perfectly well! Exactly the same way *your* baby brain fell out when you were my age. Let me guess…I know! I bet it comes out of my nose, doesn't it!? You're smiling! I knew that'd be it! It's going to come out of my nose!"

Just then Dad, who had been on his way to the bathroom, came into Millie's bedroom, switched on the light and asked:

"*What's* going to come out of your nose, Millie? Do you need a tissue?"

Dad looked a bit worried. He'd seen the sort of things that came out of Millie's nose when she had a bad cold. And it wasn't a pretty sight.

"My baby brain. It's going to fall out of my nose, just like Mum's baby brain did and your baby brain did when you were both little," replied Millie.

Mum was trying not to laugh, hiding her smile behind her hand as she spoke to Millie:

"Er, Millie…don't you think your brain might be a bit too big to just fall out of your nose?"

Millie stopped rocking her head and thought for a moment. Then she smiled and started rocking again.

"Stop messing around, Mum! I expect that being a baby brain, it's quite small, isn't it? And even if it is a bit of a tight squeeze, then it'll just be like when I came out of your tummy, won't it? You said I was a huge baby when I was born, but your…y'know…stretched a lot to let me out. That's what you said. And I expect it'll be the same with my nose, won't it?"

Mum was rocking as well now, backwards and forwards on the bed, clutching her mouth with one hand and her tummy with the other. She was trying very, very hard not to let the laughter burst out of her. Meanwhile Dad stood in the doorway, looking embarrassed.

"I'll just go and finish the washing-up," muttered Dad, his face bright red.

"What's wrong with Dad?" asked Millie, still rocking her head. "His face just went all funny. Exactly like the time I asked him why boys have willies."

"Go to sleep now, Millie. And stop that rocking! You'll make yourself dizzy," said Mum with a big grin on her face.

Downstairs in the kitchen, Dad sat at the table. He'd finished everything on the Brain Fairy's plate except for a couple of crisps, and now he was opening the cake tin.

"Clear up that mess," said Mum, looking at the crumb-covered table, banana skins, orange peel and empty beer bottle. "I don't want Millie thinking the Brain Fairy eats like a pig. And put that bottle in the recycling. I don't want Millie thinking the Brain Fairy helped herself to a beer from the fridge either."

As Dad cleaned up the table a bit, Mum told him everything Millie had said about the baby brain idea. How she'd been having trouble with her maths homework again and…well, you've already heard all that.

"I'm just hoping that she'll have forgotten all about it by morning," finished Mum as she helped herself to the two crisps that Dad had so kindly left for her.

"Especially the *stretching* bit," said Dad, shuddering a little at the thought of Millie's brain pushing its way out of her nose. "Yuk! I'm going to have nightmares about that, I just know I am!"

"You will if you eat that cheese! Come out of the fridge! You've had more than enough supper already," said Mum, throwing a banana skin at him.

But the next morning Millie certainly *hadn't* forgotten all about the baby brain business. She came down the stairs from her bedroom very fast. Not running, which Mum and Dad were always telling her not to do on the stairs. But sliding down on her bottom, which she had also been told lots of times not to do.

Slide, bump! Slide, bump! Slide, bump! Slide, bump! Slide, bump! Slide, bump! All the way to the bottom. Then she scrambled back up and slid down all over again…and again…and again…until her bottom started

to hurt and Mum stuck her head out of the bathroom door to yell:

"Stop that, Millie! We've told you a million times, you'll wear out the stair carpet doing that!"

"Sorry, Mum!" Millie shouted back from the bottom of the stairs. "I was trying to loosen my baby brain up a bit more and make it wobblier. I thought all the bumping down the stairs might help."

"Oh good grief," Millie heard Mum groan. "Well just stop it, okay?"

When Mum came down to the kitchen, the very first thing she saw was Millie, still in her pyjamas, with her finger stuck up her nose.

"Millie! Stop that! Don't pick your nose!" said Mum crossly.

But instead of stopping, Millie kept her finger firmly up her nose and continued poking around inside it.

"I'm *not* picking my nose! I'm trying to give my baby brain a poke. To see if it's getting any wobblier yet. Like I do when one of my baby teeth is getting wobbly. You know, I think it *is* wobblier than last night!"

"I need some coffee," groaned Mum. "I can't start on all that baby brain stuff again without a cup of strong coffee inside me!"

"Mum?" said Millie, taking her finger out of her nose and rubbing her sore bottom through her pyjama trousers. "Where's the arnica bruise cream? Can you put some on my bottom, please? I hurt it bumping down the stairs."

Mum filled the kettle and switched it on, then opened a drawer and started looking for the arnica cream. Meanwhile, Millie went back to poking around in her nose, trying to loosen her baby brain a bit more. When she finally pulled her finger out, after a really good poke around, there on the end of it was the largest, juiciest bogey Millie had ever seen.

"Oh well, waste not want not," she thought (that was something Granny said a lot) and popped the bogey in her mouth. "After all," she thought to herself, "if I'm going to get working on making my baby brain wobblier today, I probably won't have time for a great big breakfast!"

Mum found the bruise cream and turned to Millie, unscrewing the tube.

"Found it…what're you eating, Millie? Oh, you're not! Before breakfast? Yuk! That's disgusting!"

Dad walked in and took his favourite mug down from its shelf.

“What’re you eating, Millie?” he asked. “Did you save me some? I’m starving.”

He glanced around the kitchen, hopefully. Mum and Millie looked at each other and started laughing.

“Yes, Millie,” chuckled Mum, “don’t be so greedy. Next time, save some for Dad.”

“Okay,” giggled Millie, then she bent over so Mum could put bruise cream on her bottom.

After her (proper!) breakfast, Millie followed Dad into the sitting room. He'd plonked himself down on the settee with the newspaper and the television control. Millie's bottom had stopped hurting now, and she had another plan to help jiggle and shake her baby brain loose.

"Dad, let's play horses! We haven't done that for ages! Come on! Please!"

Dad looked a bit unsure and shook his head.

"We haven't done it for ages, Millie, because the last time we did, you were sick all over the carpet and all over the cat," he muttered, looking in the paper for the television guide.

Millie climbed up onto Dad's knee and started bouncing up and down.

"I know, Dad. But I was a lot smaller then. And I'd been eating an awful lot of chocolate and cake and jelly and trifle and custard and stuff 'cos it was my birthday. I won't be sick this time. Promise! Come on!"

Dad groaned. He remembered how the chocolate and cake and jelly and trifle and custard had all come back out of Millie and onto his trousers, onto the carpet and onto the cat in the exact opposite order to how she'd eaten them.

"Oh, all right," he said reluctantly, bouncing Millie up and down on his knee. "Clip-clop, clip-clop, clip-clop…"

Freddie the cat had been happily snoozing on the rug in front of the fireplace. But when he saw Millie bouncing on Dad's knee, he too remembered that truly horrible birthday party.

Like Dad, Freddie remembered (how could he ever forget?) Millie being sick all over Dad's trousers and all over *him.*

Leaping up from the rug in a panic, Freddie raced from the room to hide in a damp, smelly corner behind the rubbish bin in the kitchen. Anything was better than being covered in chocolate, cake, trifle and custard again, he thought. Not to mention the bath Mum had given him afterwards. He didn't know which he'd hated worse, Millie being sick on him, or all that horrible soapy water!

Back in the sitting room, Millie was bouncing faster and faster and harder and harder on Dad's knee.

"Faster!" she shouted. "Giddy-up, Dobbin! Let's go for a gallop!!"

Millie shook her head this way and that as she boinged up and down, whacking Dad's leg with her hand like a riding whip. Until, finally, she bounced right off his knee, did a wild somersault and landed with a thud on her head.

"Ouch!" said Millie, but then she thought: "Hang on! That'll help loosen up my brain even more than the bouncing up and down on Dad's knee!"

"Again, again!" she yelled, ignoring the pain in her head and clambering back onto Dad's knee. "Let's go over some jumps this time!"

Twenty minutes later, Dad was lying on the settee completely exhausted. And Millie was back in the kitchen with Mum, having bruise cream put on her *head* this time.

"Millie, you've got more bruises and carpet-grazes on your head than I can count! We're going to need a new tube of arnica. How on earth did you manage to fall off Dad's knee so many times?" asked Mum.

"It wasn't easy," said Millie. "Dad started holding onto me really tight after the first few times. So I had to do a lot of bouncing *and*

wriggling. And the last couple of times I had to bite him a bit as well, to make him let go."

"What?" said Mum, who was writing "Tube of bump cream for Millie" at the end of her shopping list on the fridge door.

"Nothing," said Millie. "Mum, can you put some more arnica on my bottom as well? It's hurting again with all that bouncing up and down."

Mum sighed and changed her shopping list to read "*Large* tube of bump cream for Millie."

Millie spent the rest of that Saturday morning trying one daft brain-loosening idea after another. She was determined to make her baby brain wobbly enough to fall out before bedtime. Partly so that the Brain Fairy could bring her the money for the new Bratz doll that very night. But mostly so that her new big-girl brain could start growing and help her to get her maths homework done before school on Monday. She was really fed up with getting rotten marks week after week.

When Mum had finished putting more bump cream on her aching bottom, Millie quickly got dressed and rushed out into the garden. There, she start boinging around like crazy on her bouncy inflatable space-hopper. It was a lot softer to bounce on than Dad's knee.

She bounced faster and faster and higher and higher. But because the space-hopper was so soft and boingey, it didn't really seem to be giving Millie's head and brain much of a shaking. Until she bounced so high that she hit the top of her head on a low branch of the old apple tree.

"Ouch!" she yelped, then thought: "But that should help loosen my baby brain quite a lot."

Back in the kitchen, Mum put more arnica cream on Millie's head and changed the shopping list again to "*Two* large tubes of bump cream for Millie."

"Try to be a bit more careful," said Mum.

"Okay," shouted Millie as she ran back outside. Then she jumped on her bike and started riding up and down the bumpiest bits of the garden path as fast as she could.

NO HANDS!

She was standing up on the pedals so that her sore bottom didn't bump on the saddle. So when her front wheel hit a particularly deep and wide crack in the path and twisted sideways, Millie flew over the handlebars and went head-first (thump!) into the wooden garden fence.

“Ouch!” she squealed, then thought “Nice one! That stupid baby brain's getting looser and wobblier all the time! I expect it'll be falling out any minute now!”

“Mum?! Is there any bump cream left?” shouted Millie. As she staggered towards the back door, she tripped over her bike and went head-first into the dustbin with yet another brain-wobbling thump.

“Ouch! Brilliant!” thought Millie as she picked herself up.

"Oh good grief!" thought Mum as she looked out of the window at Millie and reached for the arnica tube.

As soon as Mum had squeezed the very last of the bump cream onto the bruise, Millie dashed back outside and started heading her football. She hoped that would also help loosen-up her baby brain. But she'd only been at it for a minute or so when Mum ran outside to see why Millie was now yelling "Ouch, ouch, ouch, ouch, ouch, ouch, ouch, ouch…" over and over again.

"Millie! Don't be silly! You can't do headers with all those bumps and bruises!" said Mum. "Come in and help me tidy up instead."

In the house, Mum started dusting and Millie started collecting-up all her toys and dolls that were lying around, to take them back to her bedroom.

"Achoo! Achoo!" sneezed Mum as she flicked her duster over some particularly dusty ornaments. "Achoo! Oh, I really hate dusting! The dust always gets up my nose and makes me sneeze! I think I'm allergic to it! Achoo! Achoo! Good grief! Achoo! Achoo!"

Millie watched with great interest as Mum sneezed more and more loudly, her head jerking violently backwards and forwards with each little explosion of breath. Then Millie snatched the yellow duster from Mum's hand.

"Let me do it, Mum."

"Uh? Okay. Achoo! Thanks, Millie. I'll start doing the hoovering instead. Achoo!"

Flick, flick, dust, dust! Millie was making

as much dust fly from the shelves and into the air as possible.

After a minute or two of this, *her* nose started to tickle just like Mum's. And the more she flicked dust into the air, the more her nose tickled.

Until...

"Ah...ah...achoo! Achoo! Achoo!" she sneezed, thinking: "Great! This should help loosen-up my baby brain and make it wobbly. And without any bumps or bruises either!"

Flick, flick, dust, dust! The more Millie made the dust fly, the more she sneezed and the looser and wobblier she could feel her baby brain getting. Until Mum came back into the room, grabbed the duster from Millie and shooed her away from the shelves.

"Stop it, Millie! *You'll* end up with a dust allergy as well if you carry on like that. Go and hoover the hall carpet and I'll finish this," she said.

Millie went out into the hall and looked at the hoover thoughtfully for a moment. She opened the cupboard under the stairs where she knew there were some cardboard boxes. Then she fetched a pair of scissors from a drawer in the sitting room and got to work.

Five minutes later, Mum came through to see how Millie was getting on with the hoovering, only to find Millie with a cardboard box over her head. She'd cut a small round hole in the bottom of the box. And into the hole she'd shoved the hose from the hoover, so it was sucking air up through the box around Millie's head.

"Well that's one way to get rid of your nits, Millie," laughed Mum, lifting up the box. "What *are* you doing?"

"It's a baby brain sucking-out machine," answered Millie, pulling the cardboard box back down over her head.

“No, it’s a cardboard box with a hoover hose stuck in it,” said Mum. “But you stay like that while I get Dad. He won’t believe this unless he sees it. Actually, hang on while I get the video camera!”

“Don’t, Mum! It’s not funny! Stop laughing!” shouted Millie grumpily.

She pulled off the cardboard box and stomped out of the hall. When Mum caught up with her, Millie was back in the garden, pulling herself up onto her climbing frame.

“Seriously, Millie,” said Mum. “No more brain-bumping, brain-shaking, brain-poking or brain-sucking, okay? You’re covered in bruises and you’re going to really hurt yourself if you carry on like this. Plus, that arnica bump cream isn't cheap, and you've got through a whole tube in one morning.”

“Yeah, okay. I’ve probably loosened my baby brain up enough now anyway. I’ll just hang around and wait for it to fall out,” replied Millie.

And hang around is exactly what Millie did. She hooked her legs over a bar of the climbing frame and dangled upside-down with her arms folded, waiting for her wobbly baby brain to fall out.

"Now what are you doing," demanded Mum when she came out half an hour later to tell Millie that lunch was ready. "Why are you still hanging there like that?"

“I'm waiting for my baby brain to drop out,” said Millie. “It’ll probably come away quicker if I hang with my head down. What? I’m not bumping or poking or shaking or sucking or anything! I’m just *waiting*. What’s wrong with that?”

“Well come on in. Lunch is on the table,” said Mum.

“I’m not hungry,” said Millie, and started hiccupping loudly, which she always did when she got hungry. “Good!” she thought to herself. “That’ll help make my baby brain come loose too!”

“Suit yourself,” replied Mum, going back inside to talk to Dad. She had a worried look on her face now.

“This can’t go on any longer,” said Mum as she and Dad stared out of the kitchen window at Millie, hanging upside-down from the climbing frame. “We’re going to have to tell Millie this baby brain business is a load of silly nonsense. She’s going to be very disappointed and upset, but…"

Mum stopped talking and looked at a bowl of mixed nuts on the kitchen worktop.

"…hmmm, that might work though," she said, thoughtfully.

"What?" said Dad. "Tell her it's all stupid nonsense? Okay, I'll do it."

Mum took a shelled walnut from the bowl and looked at it.

"No. Just hang on a minute. Get me Millie's paint box. I've got an idea," said Mum.

"What are you doing?" asked Dad as he watched Mum carefully paint the walnut a pale grey colour.

"It's lucky Alfie's staying at his friend's house all weekend," said Mum as she painted. "If he knew what was going on, *he'd* certainly have no problem telling Millie how silly she's being. In fact he'd have great fun telling her. And teasing her about it. Even though he's the one who started it, telling Millie she's got a tiny baby brain. Just don't tell him *anything* about all this when he gets back. Okay?"

Dad nodded as Mum blew gently on the grey-painted nut to dry it.

"There," she said, holding the grey nut under Dad's nose. "Doesn't that look like a little brain? A *baby brain*?"

"I suppose it does a bit," said Dad, looking puzzled. Then a brilliant idea hit him. "Hey! You know what? We could pretend to Millie that this is *her* baby brain. And that it's fallen out just like she's been saying it would…"

Mum was holding the grey-painted nut and looking at Dad patiently. Dad stopped talking, looked at the nut and then looked at Mum.

"Oh, you'd already thought of that, hadn't you?" he said.

Mum nodded.

"Yes. If she thinks her baby brain's fallen out and her big-girl brain is growing in its place, that might make her think she *can* do her maths homework instead of always thinking she *can't* do it," said Mum.

"Maybe it'll give her the confidence she needs to start understanding her maths. And to start remembering her spellings. It's worth a try anyway. And when she gets older, we can tell her the truth and we'll all have a good laugh about it."

"You wait here," she said to Dad, and marched out into the garden, the grey walnut clenched in her hand behind her back.

"Ooh, look, Millie! Doesn't that cloud look just like a giraffe? Look! That one there," she said, pointing at the sky.

Millie stared up at the clouds, trying very hard to spot one that looked like a giraffe.

?
FLICK!

But of course there wasn't one. And while Millie was looking up, Mum quickly dropped the grey walnut into the long grass near the old apple tree, where Millie had banged the top of her head.

"Hey, Millie!" exclaimed Mum, pointing down at the grass. "What's that?! It looks like… no! I can't believe it! Can it be…do you know, I think it *is*…"

“It's my baby brain!!” screeched Millie excitedly. “It must have come out of my nose when I bumped my head on that branch, and I didn’t even notice!”

“Great!” said Mum, waving her hands in the air excitedly. “Fantastic! I can hardly believe it! My little girl’s baby brain has fallen out! Oh, you’re going to be so clever when your big-girl brain grows in. You’ll be able to do maths and spellings like there’s nothing to them! This is so great! And we can put your baby brain under your pillow tonight for the Brain Fairy. How much did you say you were hoping she’d give you? Five pounds?”

“Eight pounds ninety-five pence. But hang on, Mum!” said Millie, sounding a little worried. “What if my big-girl brain takes a long time to grow? Like my proper teeth took ages to grow after my two front baby teeth fell out, and I had a big gap for ages? What if I have a gap in my *head*?! Then I’d be even *worse* at maths and spellings!”

Mum looked anxiously towards the house where Dad was peering out of the kitchen window. He smiled encouragingly and gave Mum a thumbs-up sign. She sighed, reached down and gently tapped Millie on the head with the knuckles of her fingers.

"Does that sound *hollow*?" she asked.

Millie closed her eyes and concentrated hard.

"Do it again!" she said.

Mum did, gently but firmly rapping Millie on the forehead.

"No!" said Millie, opening her eyes and smiling. "It *doesn't* sound hollow! I *don't* have a gappy head! My big-girl brain must be growing in already!"

"Yes," said Mum. "Like when a baby tooth falls out, sometimes you can see the new tooth starting to come through underneath. That's what's happening. Phew! Lucky you! That's a relief, isn't it?!"

Millie swung down off the climbing frame as Mum bent down and picked up the painted walnut from the grass.

"I'll take this," said Mum, carefully wrapping the grey nut in a tissue from her pocket. "I'll put it under your pillow when you go to bed."

"You know," said Millie brightly, "I think I'm going to manage my maths homework okay from now on…and my spellings! I can feel my new big-girl brain making me brainier and brainier all the time! I'm so happy, Mum!"

Mum felt a tear welling up in her eye and a lump in her throat as she realised just how happy and relieved her little girl was feeling right now. After all the weeks and months of struggling with her homework.

Then Millie looked up at Mum and said: "Mum? When will my baby *eyes* fall out?"

“What?” gasped Mum.

“When will my baby *eyes* fall out and my big-girl eyes grow? Then I can watch all those scary films and TV programmes that Alfie watches and I’m not allowed to. Like the scary bits in the Harry Potter films. I can’t wait for that! I’m really fed up with Alfie telling me I can’t watch what he’s watching on the telly ‘cos it’s not suitable for my little baby-girl eyes!”

That night, as Millie lay in bed fast asleep, dreaming about the Brain Fairy and Bratz dolls, Dad crept into her bedroom. He slipped his hand under Millie’s pillow and found the ‘baby brain’ walnut, still wrapped in tissue, where Mum had put it at bedtime. Very carefully, so as not to wake Millie, he slid it out and replaced it with a little envelope containing eight pounds ninety-five pence.

Down in the kitchen, Mum was sitting at the table carefully painting bright blue circles on a pair of white ping-pong balls. As Dad came in with the grey walnut in his hand, Mum put two black dots in the middle of the blue circles.

"Why are you painting those table-tennis balls to look like eyes?" asked Dad, putting the painted walnut in the rubbish bin.

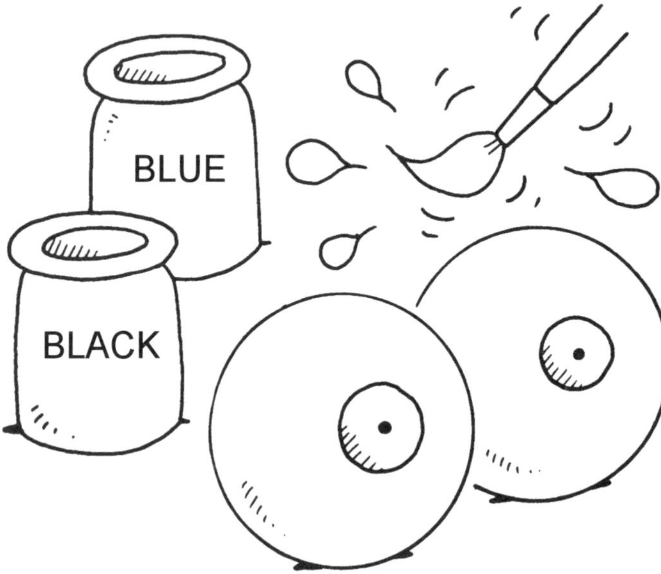

"You really don't want to know," said Mum.

Upstairs, Millie had stopped dreaming about the Brain Fairy. As she slept, her hand crept under her pillow and found the envelope with the Bratz doll money. She smiled in her sleep and started to dream instead about the Eyeball Fairy coming to collect her baby eyes.

In her dream, she was working out exactly how much baby eyes should be worth if she only had two of them but she had lots of baby teeth worth 50p each. The problem was to work out how much each baby eye was worth if both baby eyes were equal to all her baby teeth put together.

After all, both her baby eyes might not fall out at the same time. One might fall out one day, and the other might go all wobbly and drop out another day. So she needed to know exactly how much to ask the Eyeball Fairy for both eyes together *or* for first one baby eye and then the other.

At first Millie thought it was going to be a very, very difficult maths problem indeed. But the more she dreamed about it, the easier it got, until the answer was just…easy peasy.

The End

AN EXTRA BIT OF BOOK FREE!

As you've been very good and read all the way to the end of the story, we've decided to give you an extra bit of book absolutely free! No additional charge at all.

The next four pages are a special extra feature. They're an 'out-take' from the story. Just like the out-takes you sometimes find at the end of a DVD or video tape of a film. Bits of the film that were left out because they weren't quite right, didn't really fit in, had silly mistakes in them, or something like that. You know the kind of thing.

Well, this out-take is a bit of the book that we really liked, but it just didn't fit in anywhere in the story. So here it is...

Alfie's favourite joke.

No, you'll pull the flush
like everyone else!

I don't get it!

And there's no cake mixture in this bowl!
It's just a prop.

ABOUT THE AUTHOR AND ILLUSTRATOR

Martin Baxendale has been a writer and cartoonist all his life. His funny gift-books for grown-ups have sold millions of copies in Britain and lots of other countries too.

His best-known grown-ups' book is one called YOUR NEW BABY - AN OWNER'S MANUAL. Maybe your Mum or your Dad read it when *you* were a baby?

As well as writing and illustrating books, Martin used to draw cartoon strips for children's comics, just like his Dad, Leo Baxendale, who is famous for inventing the Bash Street Kids and Minnie The Minx strips for the Beano comic. He also used to draw cartoons for greeting cards, has written books about gardening, and before all that was once a newspaper reporter.

Martin lives in Gloucestershire with his wife and children, a cat called Mitzi and a pet worm called Brian (okay, we made that last bit up. His pet worm's really called Fred).

He says he likes making children laugh (and then pinching their sweets when they're not looking).